This book belongs to:

For Mama B, whose kanga nurtured me.
Love M.

Mama's Magical Kanga © Maria G.N. Biswalo 2021.
Illustrations © Theresia Mmasi 2021.
ISBN 978-3-949620-00-3

Mama's Magical Kanga

WRITTEN BY

Maria G.N. Biswalo

ILLUSTRATED BY

Theresia Mmasi

WOOAAW

My mama's kanga is magical.

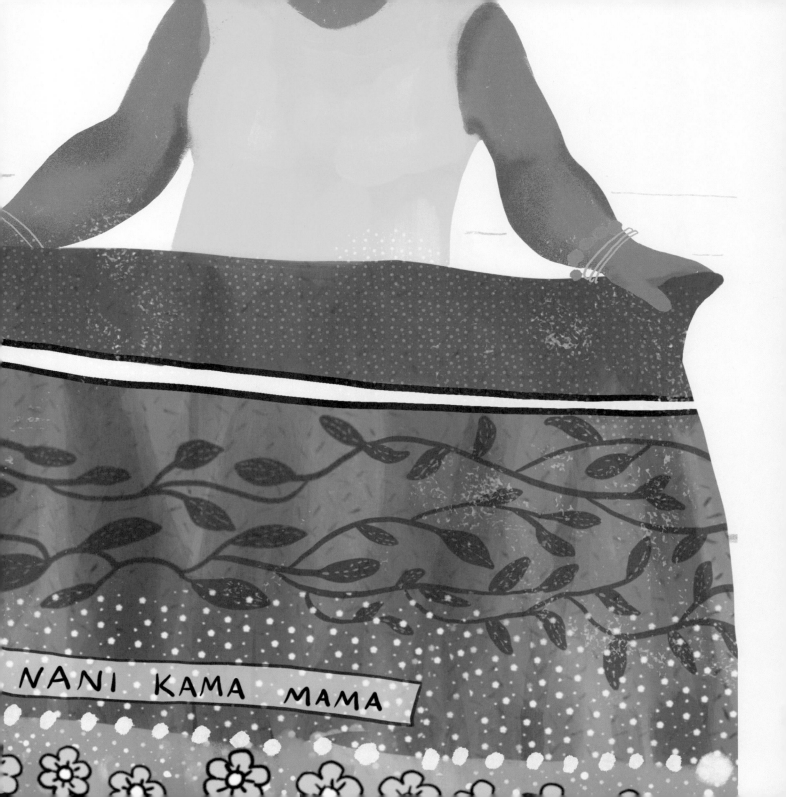

Mama's kanga carries me...

and plays with me too.

Mama's kanga
washes me...

and dries me too.

Mama's kanga diapers me...

and cuddles me too.

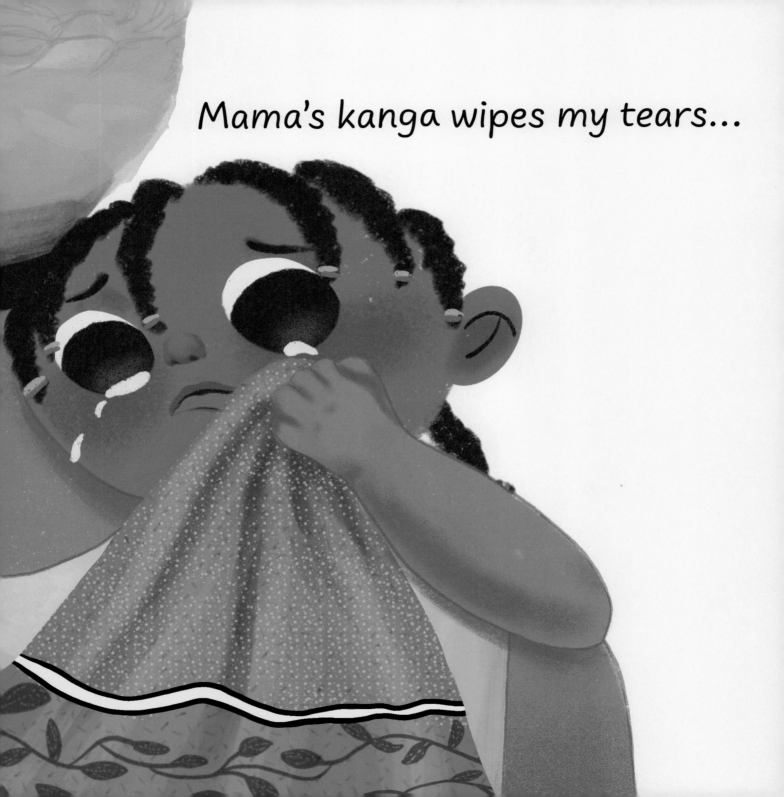

Mama's kanga wipes my tears...

and comforts me too.

Mama's kanga can be anything
I want it to be...

I can fly high.

I can explore far and wide.

I can tumble
and get back up.

I can score a winning goal.

but MY favourite
is when…

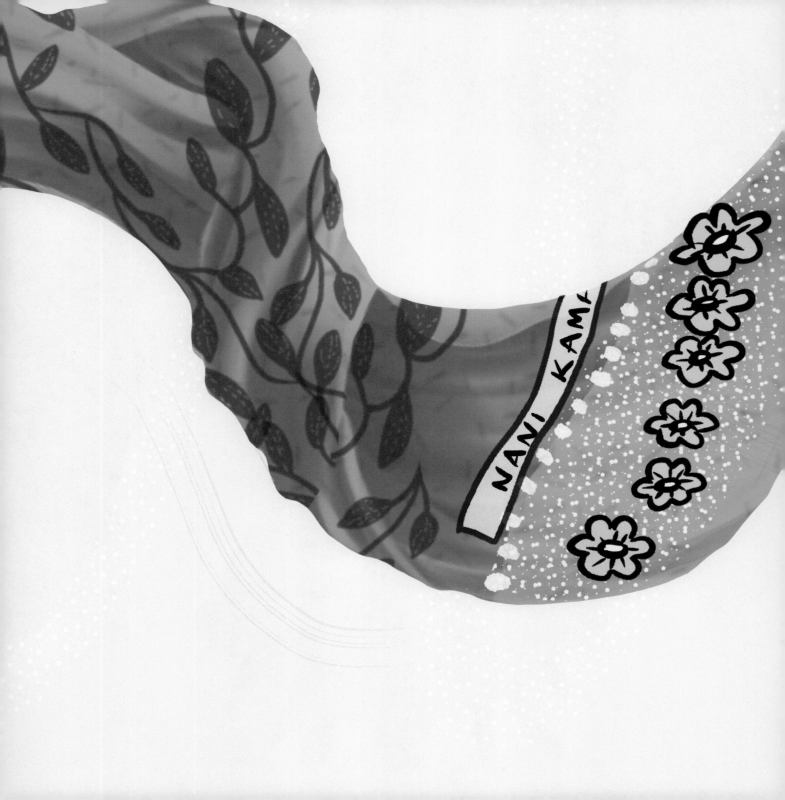

Mama's kanga
dresses HER...

NANI KAMA MAMA

and dresses ME too!

What is a kanga?

A kanga is a multipurpose piece of fabric that is worn throughout East Africa and especially around the coastal regions.

A kanga is rectangular and usually has a border and words written on it. These words range from proverbs to musings that are meant to deliver a message to the community.

NOTE FROM THE AUTHOR
ABOUT SHARED READING

Reading and listening to stories should be an enjoyable and interactive activity. Allow children to ask questions during and after the shared storytelling. This gives them a chance to make meaning and connect to the pictures and texts. Encourage both realistic and whimsical musings, and most of all, enjoy diving into the story.

 SOME GUIDING QUESTIONS TO HELP YOU ALONG

What was the most interesting thing you learned from the book?
What was your favourite part of the story?
Why do you think the author wrote this book?
Does this book remind you of anything else you've already read or seen?
What kinds of things can you/ we make and create to share about what you read in *Mama's Magical Kanga*?
If you had a *kanga*, what would you do with it?
Do you have something at home that is like a *kanga*? Can it be used in many ways?

MARIA G. N. BISWALO
THE AUTHOR

As an international educator and mother to bi-cultural children, Maria G. N. Biswalo noted a lack of representation in early literacy texts that depicted her Tanzanian culture and mother tongue- Kiswahili/Swahili. Through her stories, Maria hopes to bridge that gap and inspire more stories from her motherland to emerge and be easily accessed across the globe. She invites you to connect with her at *www.hadithizamama.com*

THERESIA MMASI
THE ILLUSTRATOR

A Tanzanian multidisciplinary designer with a love for illustration, history and art education, Theresia regards herself as a creative thinker, maker and doer. Pursuing work with the goal to create for a more inclusive, sustainable and just world, she believes that graphic design can provide people in underserved communities with visual tools to own and tell their own stories.